JAMESTOWN EDUCATION

Reading Fluency

Reader

Level
I
9

Camille L. Z. Blachowicz, Ph.D.

McGraw Hill Glencoe

New York, New York   Columbus, Ohio   Chicago, Illinois   Peoria, Illinois   Woodland Hills, California

JAMESTOWN ⛵ EDUCATION

Glencoe

The *McGraw·Hill* Companies

Send all inquiries to:
Glencoe/McGraw-Hill
8787 Orion Place
Columbus, OH 43240-4027

ISBN 0-07-845699-1
Printed in the United States of America.
1 2 3 4 5 6 7 8 9 10 021 09 08 07 06 05 04 03

Contents

⚬⚬⚬

The passages in this book are taken from the following sources.

How to Use These Books

The Reading Fluency *Reader* contains 72 reading passages. The accompanying *Reader's Record* contains two copies of each of these passages and includes a place for marking *miscues*.

What Procedure Do I Follow?

1. Read a selection from the *Reader* as your partner marks any miscues you make on the corresponding page in your *Reader's Record*. (A miscue is a reading error. See explanation in How to Use These Books in the *Reader's Record*.) The recorder's job is to listen carefully and make a tick mark above each place in the text where a miscue occurs, and to make a slash mark indicating where you stop reading after "Time!" is called.

2. The recorder says when to start and calls "Time!" after a minute.

3. After the reading, the recorder

   • counts the number of words read, using the number guides at the right-hand side of the passage in the *Reader's Record,* and records the Total Words Read

   • writes the total number of miscues for each line in the far right-hand column labeled Miscues. Totals and records the miscues on the Total Errors line

   • subtracts Total Errors from Total Words Read to find the Correct Words Per Minute (WPM) and records that score on the Correct WPM line

4. Review the *Reader's Record,* noting your miscues. Discuss with your partner the characteristics of good reading you have displayed. Then rate your own performance and mark the scale at the bottom of the page.

5. Change roles with your partner and repeat the procedure.

6. You and your partner then begin a second round of reading the same passage. When it is your turn to read, try to improve in pace, expression, and accuracy over the first reading.

7. After completing two readings, record your Correct WPM scores in the back of your *Reader's Record*. Follow the directions on the graph.

1

Nonfiction

from *Woman in the Mists:*
The Story of Dian Fossey and the
Mountain Gorillas of Africa
by Farley Mowat

Today Sanweke and I were charged by two gorillas and it wasn't a bluff charge—they really meant it. We were about one hundred and fifty feet directly downhill from a group when a silverback and a female decided to eradicate us. They gave us a split second of warning with screams and roars that seemed to come from every direction at once before they descended in a gallop that shook the ground. I was determined to stand fast, but when they broke through the foliage at a dead run directly above me, I felt my legs retreating in spite of what I've read about gorillas not charging fully. I paused long enough to try to dissuade them with my voice, which only seemed to aggravate them more, if possible; and when their long, yellow canines and wild eyes were no less than two feet away, I took a very ungainly nosedive into the thick foliage alongside the trail. They whizzed on by, caught up in their own momentum. It's a good thing they didn't come back to attack, for I was certainly in no position to defend myself. It may have taken only a split second to dive into that foliage, but it took about fifteen minutes to extract myself—what a tangle!

Pronunciation Guide

eradicate: i rad′ ə kāt′   dissuade: di swād′

from *The Mysterious Island*
by Jules Verne

A balloon was being swept along by a hurricane at a speed of more than a hundred miles an hour. In the basket swinging below it were five passengers. The air between them and the surface of the water was filled with heavy mist.

Where had that balloon come from? The hurricane had been raging for five days and the balloon could not have traveled less than two thousand miles every twenty-four hours, so it must have come from very far away.

In any case, the passengers had no way of knowing how far they had come. Moving at the same speed as the wind, they did not feel it. The mist around them was so thick that they could not even tell if it was night or day. The balloon had stayed so high that they had not been able to see or hear anything below them. Only now, when they had begun sinking rapidly, did they realize that they were in danger of falling into the ocean.

When they had lightened the balloon by throwing out their weapons, ammunition, food and supplies, it rose to an altitude of forty-five hundred feet.

They spent the night in terrible anxiety. At dawn the storm began to show signs of dying down. By eleven o'clock the mist was gone and the wind was less strong. But the balloon was again sinking.

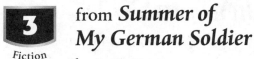

3

Fiction

from *Summer of My German Soldier*

by Bette Greene

Jimmy Wells pointed to the last passenger car. "There!"

Everyone hurried toward the end of the train in time to see two GIs with their side arms still strapped in their holsters step quickly from the car. Then came the Germans. The crowd moved back slightly, leaving a one-person-wide path between themselves and the train.

The prisoners were unhandcuffed, unchained young men carrying regulation Army duffel bags. They wore fresh blue denim pants and matching shirts, and if it hadn't been for the black "POW" stenciled across their shirt backs you could easily have mistaken them for an ordinary crew from the Arkansas Public Works Department sent out to repair a stretch of highway. I tried to read their faces for brutality, terror, humiliation—something. But the only thing I sensed was a kind of relief at finally having arrived at their destination.

"Nazis!" A woman's voice shouted. And this time I knew for sure that it was Mrs. Benn.

A blond prisoner who was stepping off the train at that moment stopped short then smiled and waved. It was as though he believed, or wanted to believe, that Mrs. Benn's call was nothing more than a friendly American greeting.

I raised my hand, but before I completed a full wave Mary Wren pressed it down, shaking her head.

from *Lift Every Voice*

by Dorothy Sterling and Benjamin Quarles

Hampton—its full name was Hampton Normal and Agricultural Institute—was one of a group of schools for Negroes established after the Civil War. In addition to book-learning, General Samuel Armstrong, Hampton's founder, taught his pupils the niceties of daily living that they had had no chance to learn under slavery.

[Booker T. Washington's] first lesson came on the night of his arrival when he was given a bed to sleep in. Should he crawl under the sheets? Lie on top of them? Only after watching the other boys did he decide to sleep in between. Lesson number two was the toothbrush, lesson number three the tablecloth. For the first time in his sixteen years, the son of the plantation cook sat down at a table to eat, and used a napkin, knife, and fork.

Booker spent three happy years at Hampton. Supporting himself by working as the janitor, he learned everything that the school had to offer—geography, grammar, history, science, and practical instruction in farming and handicrafts. A teacher gave him private lessons in public speaking, drilling him until he spoke clearly and emphasized important words in order to hold the interest of his audience. He became a leader in Hampton's debating society and a commencement speaker at his graduation.

from *Trial by Ice*

by K. M. Kostyal

Shackleton had hoped that a vast plain of snow and ice lay between him and [the South Pole]. But he was wrong. The high, jagged Transantarctic Mountains stood in his path. But luck was on his side. In early December he and his men came upon one of the few passes through the mountains. A glacier they called the Golden Gateway led them to a stupendous ice field 30 miles wide and more than 100 miles long. [One of the men] believed that it "must be the largest in the world. . . ." Though deep snow, crevasses, and other obstacles marred its glistening blue surface, still it beckoned like a wide road, and Shackleton and his men took it.

A week later they were still climbing the glacier, scrambling over high ridges of ice, roped together to keep from falling into hidden crevasses. As they climbed higher, the cold and wind grew worse, and frostbite threatened their fingers, toes, and faces. They were running low on food and had little fuel left either to cook with or to melt snow for drinking water. Yet they kept going, and by December 28 they at last left the glacier behind and became the first humans ever to set foot on the smooth, vast ice cap that covers the South Pole.

Pronunciation Guide

crevasses: krə vas′ ez

Thirteen Days in October

John F. Kennedy, President of the United States, peered at the photographs taken by a U–2 spy plane flying high over Cuba. Nikita Khrushchev, premier of the Soviet Union, was installing offensive nuclear weapons just 90 miles off the Florida coast. It was October 15, 1962.

Kennedy called his advisers together. Some favored an immediate air strike and an invasion of Cuba; some thought the United States should put up a naval blockade around Cuba to turn away Soviet ships carrying weapons. Finally Kennedy decided. The navy would put up a blockade.

Then on October 26, Kennedy received a letter from Khrushchev proposing that the Soviets would remove the missiles in exchange for a U.S. pledge never to invade Cuba. Before Kennedy could reply, a second Khrushchev letter arrived proposing a different solution. Khrushchev wanted U.S. missiles in Turkey removed in exchange for the removal of the Cuban missiles.

The terms of Khrushchev's first letter were acceptable, but not the terms of the second. So Kennedy ignored the second letter. He answered the first letter instead. He replied on October 27th, and the next day a message came from Khrushchev. Yes, the Soviet Union would accept the terms as stated in the President's letter. Somehow during those 13 days in October 1962, a war was avoided.

Pronunciation Guide

Nikita Khrushchev: ni kē' tə   kro͞osh chef

from *Norby and the Oldest Dragon*

by Janet and Isaac Asimov

Cadet Jefferson Wells was having a difficult time packing his suitcase because his room at Space Academy was crowded with three other cadets bubbling with curiosity and questions about Jeff's secret destination.

Norby was no help, either. Although he didn't ask questions because he knew where they were going, he was trying to impress the other cadets with the fact that he was an efficient personal robot in spite of being small, barrel-shaped, and having only half a head. Waving his extensible arms, Norby gave advice. Lots of advice.

"Jeff, don't put your spare boots on the bottom because everything on top will get lumpy. Put them into the spaces left when you've finished everything else. And don't forget to pack your new toothpastebrush because the one in the suitcase is empty. And I recommend at least two extra pairs of socks because the last time we went anywhere you didn't even have one to change into . . ."

As Norby droned on and the other cadets laughed, Jeff rebelliously put in only one extra pair of socks. After all, they were only going for the weekend.

Although he was an orphaned fifteen-year-old, Jeff had managed to survive many dubious adventures, most of them caused by the fact that his so-called teaching robot contained weird alien parts and mixed everything up at unexpected moments.

8

Fiction

from *The Great Interactive Dream Machine*

by Richard Peck

Something had scared [the dog] under the furniture, and I thought I knew what.

I followed the smell of a small electrical fire down a long hall to [my best friend] Aaron's room.

I pushed open his door. He's got a bed in there and a stack of *Byte* magazines from the school media center, and a book called *Navigating the Internet.* But the rest of the room is an ultra-high-tech, state-of-the-art, stand-alone microsystem workstation.

It's built around a pair of Big Blue's power PC's with a couple of high-definition TV screens and more add-ons and video assets than you can believe. We're talking mainframe here. It goes to the ceiling, with wires and cables snaking around the floor. Aaron calls it his personalized blendo-technopolis. He uses terms like this, and I don't know what they mean.

As late as last winter if Aaron wanted to [experiment with] his data on two keyboards at once, he had to use the computers in the school media center. We were both *this close* to getting in big trouble for being in there when we weren't supposed to be. Now I noticed that his home workstation had doubled in size.

from *An Ocean Apart, a World Away*

by Lensey Namioka

One Saturday, the [Pettigrew family] invited me to go with them to a football game between Cornell and Yale. I was astounded by the loud yells of the spectators. It sounded like a revolution breaking out, except that what I had seen of the revolution in China had not been quite so noisy.

Nor could I make any sense of the game, since all I could see was a big muddle, with the players crashing into one another. Having possession of the ball was apparently very important, but I never did catch a glimpse of it. At least I could tell which players were on our side and which were against us: The Cornell boys wore red, and the Yale boys wore blue.

Suddenly there was a huge roar, and all the spectators around me jumped to their feet. From the yells, I gathered that someone had downed a touch—or maybe touched a down. Whatever it was, it was obviously a good thing.

After the roaring died down, somebody blew a whistle, and the players left the field. A file of musicians playing various instruments marched across the field, reminding me of an old-fashioned Chinese funeral.

"It's halftime," said Mr. Pettigrew. When I didn't understand, he explained. "It's like an intermission. Boy, I can use a rest from all this excitement."

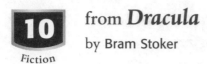

from *Dracula*

by Bram Stoker

Fiction

"You know this place, Jonathan. You have copied maps of it, and you know it at least more than we do. Which is the way to the chapel?" I had an idea of its direction, though on my former visit I had not been able to get admission to it; so I led the way, and after a few wrong turnings found myself opposite a low, arched oaken door, ribbed with iron bands. "This is the spot," said the Professor as he turned his lamp on a small map of the house, copied from the file of my original correspondence regarding the purchase. With a little trouble we found the key on the bunch and opened the door. We were prepared for some unpleasantness, for as we were opening the door a faint, malodorous air seemed to exhale through the gaps, but none of us ever expected such an odor as we encountered. None of the others had met the Count at all at close quarters, and when I had seen him he was either in the fasting stage of his existence in his rooms or, when he was gloated with fresh blood, in a ruined building open to the air; but here the place was small and close, and the long disuse had made the air stagnant and foul.

11

Fiction

from *The Hound of the Baskervilles*

by Arthur Conan Doyle

Mr. Sherlock Holmes, who was usually very late in the mornings, save upon those not infrequent occasions when he was up all night, was seated at the breakfast table. I stood upon the hearth-rug and picked up the stick which our visitor had left behind him the night before. It was a fine, thick piece of wood, bulbous-headed, of the sort which is known as a "Penang lawyer." Just under the head was a broad silver band, nearly an inch across. "To James Mortimer, M.R.C.S., from his friends of the C.C.II.," was engraved upon it, with the date "1884." It was just such a stick as the old-fashioned family practitioner used to carry—dignified, solid, and reassuring.

"Well, Watson, what do you make of it?"

Holmes was sitting with his back to me, and I had given him no sign of my occupation.

"How did you know what I was doing? I believe you have eyes in the back of your head."

"I have, at least, a well-polished silver plated coffee-pot in front of me," said he. "But, tell me, Watson, what do you make of our visitor's stick? Since we have been so unfortunate as to miss him and have no notion of his errand, this accidental souvenir becomes of importance. Let me hear you reconstruct the man by an examination of it."

Pronunciation Guide

bulbous: bul′ bəs   Penang: pē′ nang′

from *The Buried City of Pompeii*

by Shelley Tanaka

Vesuvius erupted on August 24, A.D. 79. [The city of] Pompeii had been experiencing earth tremors for a few days, and many people still remembered an earthquake that had damaged much of the city seventeen years before. But they did not realize that they were living in the lap of a deadly volcano.

At about 1 P.M., the mountain roared, and her summit cracked open. A huge column of pumice and ash shot up into the air like a rocket. When the column reached the height of 12 miles, it spread out like a fountain. Ash and pumice began to fall to the ground.

In horror, the people of Pompeii had to decide whether to flee or stay. Most chose to run, and soon the gates were clogged with humans and pack animals trying to push their way out of the city. Others hid in their homes, hoping that by some miracle, the rain of fire would soon stop.

But it didn't. With every passing hour, another 6 inches of pumice covered Pompeii. By late afternoon, the sky was almost black. Roofs caved in. Walls collapsed as earth tremors rocked the city.

At midnight, the column of ash and pumice finally collapsed back to earth. That's when superhot rock and gas spewed up out of the volcano and began to flow down the mountain, smothering and burning up the countryside.

Pronunciation Guide

pumice: **pum′ is**

from *Turn of the Century*
by Nancy Smiler Levinson

One night in July 1881, fifteen-year-old Kate Shelley and her mother stood anxiously looking through a window of their Iowa farmhouse. Outside a raging storm was swelling the waters of Honey Creek, which emptied into the swiftly flowing Des Moines River.

They had already rescued the livestock from the flooded barn and moved the animals to higher ground, and they had calmed the frightened younger children in their beds. But the storm grew worse, and their worries heightened.

Nearby lay the tracks of the Chicago and Northwestern Railroad, where Kate's father, an Irish immigrant, had worked as a section foreman before he died in an accident on the job. About eleven o'clock, Kate and her mother heard an engine whistle. But no train was scheduled in either direction at that hour. Suddenly, they heard a crash and the hissing of steam. They knew at once what had happened.

The No. 11, an engine from the Moingona station, had been sent ahead to check the track's safety for an express passenger train scheduled to pass through at midnight. The Honey Creek wooden bridge had been washed out, and the No. 11 had plunged into the river below.

The women were horrified. Kate knew she had to help the men and get word to the station operator to stop the midnight train.

Pronunciation Guide

Moingona: moin gō′ nə

from *Keepers and Creatures at the National Zoo*

by Peggy Thomson

First thing, keeper Morna Holden has her heart in her mouth as she greets and good-mornings everyone on her line in the Elephant House—the two Asian elephants, the rhino, and especially African elephant Nancy, who was sick yesterday.

Today Nancy is herself again—clear-eyed and alert. Morna expected her to be. All the same, she's relieved. She tells Nancy as much while she hoists herself into the enclosure to run a hand over Nancy's waving trunk and her fanning ears and to hug a foreleg. In the fond, grumbling way of an elephant keeper to an elephant, she complains about an animal's pigging out on junk food, for that's what she suspects Nancy did.

Yesterday Morna found the elephant flopped out flat, and the first times she'd gotten Nancy up and standing, all four and a half tons of her, Nancy'd sunk to her knees and flopped again. Indigestion, by the look of it, an elephant-sized bellyache, which doesn't happen often but happens. Nancy has a way of reaching out her trunk over the rail and accepting all-wrong gifts from the public. She'd been at it on Saturday. In the past she's taken candies, wrappers, mittens, cartons. Not hamburgers—she rejects them. Once, according to her keepers, she downed a backpack, though elephant keepers have been known to exaggerate.

15

Fiction

from *Mountain Light*

by Laurence Yep

I recognized the Stranger, Yammer. One moment he was running with his fists pumping at the air, and the next moment he was flying through the air and sprawling in the dirt.

He scrambled to his feet almost immediately, and we could see that his face was so contorted by fear that it no longer seemed quite human. His lips were twisted back to reveal his teeth, and his eyelids were drawn up so that his eyes were whiter and wider than a normal human's. He took one step and fell with a grunt.

He rolled over onto his back as he raised one leg and clasped his ankle. He squinted in pain as if he had twisted it on some unseen root. And suddenly the torchlight was bright beneath us as the other villagers surrounded the Stranger.

His eyes opened in terror and he gave a start—as if he saw us hiding in the branches of the tree, but the villagers were too occupied with him to turn around and notice us. I thought for a moment that he might try to save himself by turning us in as spies or something; but he kept silent, though the villagers narrowed the ring around him.

from *On the Bus with Joanna Cole: A Creative Autobiography*

by Joanna Cole, with Wendy Saul

My father was a very intelligent man who could do just about anything, but he didn't think of himself as intelligent. That's because he had dyslexia and never could read very well as a child. In those days, people didn't know about dyslexia, and his teachers punished and shamed him for it. Later in life he taught himself to read the newspaper, but he never became a real reader.

One day, when I was about twelve or thirteen, I was lying on the sofa immersed in a novel. My father came by and asked with genuine curiosity, "What is it like to read a book like that?" I told him about the experience of reading—about how the words on the page seem to disappear and you become lost in the story, seeing pictures and hearing voices in your head. I felt a new appreciation of an intense pleasure that I had simply taken for granted before and sorry that my father could not share it.

You might think that a man who did not read or write very much could not be a strong influence on a writer. But that isn't true at all of my father and me. He was a fabulous storyteller.

Pronunciation Guide

dyslexia: dis lek′ sē ə

from *Eleanor Roosevelt: A Life of Discovery*

by Russell Freedman

Never before had the American people seen a First Lady like Eleanor Roosevelt. Soon she was flying off all over the country, serving as her husband's personal investigative reporter and gathering material for her columns, articles, radio talks, and books. Reporters who covered the White House and traveled with Mrs. Roosevelt marveled at her energy and pace.

She was a frequent flier at a time when a trip in an airplane was considered a great adventure. Once, in order to impress the public with the ease and safety of air travel, Amelia Earhart invited the First Lady to join her on a flight from Washington to Baltimore. They both wore evening dresses. "How do you feel being piloted by a woman?" Eleanor was asked. "Absolutely safe," she replied. "I'd give a lot to do it myself!"

Eleanor seemed to go everywhere. Since she could travel more freely than Franklin, she again became his "eyes and ears." She dropped in on coal miners in Appalachia, slum-dwellers in Puerto Rico, and sharecroppers in their tarpaper shacks in southern cotton fields. And she inspected government relief projects from one end of the country to the other, "often managing to arrive without advance notice so that they could not be polished up for my inspection."

Pronunciation Guide

Appalachia: ap′ ə lāch′ ə

from *Behind Barbed Wire:*
The Imprisonment of Japanese
Americans During World War II
by Daniel S. Davis

Early in January 1942, the Justice Department caved in to military pressure and agreed to stricter controls on enemy aliens. This included spot raids on their homes.

Soon, FBI agents raided homes of Japanese residents. They peppered them with questions about their loyalty and searched for forbidden items.

The raids sparked a new wave of fear in the Japanese community. People who had kept mementos of the old country now followed the lead of those who had destroyed them just after Pearl Harbor. Many . . . wives [of Japanese citizens living in the U.S.] packed traveling bags for their husbands, so that if the FBI took them away in the dead of night, they would have a fresh change of clothes and toilet articles with them.

Hundreds of FBI agents trundled out of Japanese neighborhoods loaded down with cartons of contraband— items enemy aliens were forbidden to have in their possession. These included cameras; knives, including Boy Scout hunting knives; and explosives sometimes used by farmers. The results of these raids could easily have been predicted. Attorney General Biddle reported to the president:

"We have not uncovered through these searches any dangerous persons that we could not otherwise know about."

from "A White Heron"
by Sarah Orne Jewett

Sylvia felt her way easily. She had often climbed there, and knew that higher still one of the oak's upper branches chafed against the pine trunk, just where its lower boughs were set close together. There, when she made the dangerous pass from one tree to the other, the great enterprise would really begin.

She crept out along the swaying oak limb at last, and took the daring step across into the old pine tree. The way was harder than she thought; she must reach far and hold fast. The sharp dry twigs caught and held her and scratched her like angry talons, the pitch made her thin little fingers clumsy and stiff as she went round and round the tree's great stem, higher and higher upward. The sparrows and robins in the woods below were beginning to wake and twitter to the dawn, yet it seemed much lighter there aloft in the pine tree, and the child knew she must hurry if her project were to be of any use.

The tree seemed to lengthen itself out as she went up, and to reach farther and farther upward. It was like a great mainmast to the voyaging earth.

20

Fiction

from *So Big*

by Edna Ferber

The historic old Haymarket on west Randolph Street had
become the stand for market gardeners for miles around
Chicago. Here they stationed their wagons in preparation
for the next day's selling. The wagons stood, close packed,
in triple rows, down both sides of the curb and in the
middle of the street. The early comer got the advantageous
stand. There was no regular allotment of space. Pervus
tried to reach the Haymarket by nine at night. Often
bad roads made a detour necessary and he was late.
That usually meant bad business next day. The men, for
the most part, slept on their wagons, curled up on the
wagon-seat or stretched out on the sacks. Their horses
were stabled and fed in nearby sheds, with more actual
comfort than the men themselves. One could get a room
for twenty-five cents in one of the ramshackle rooming
houses that faced the street. But the rooms were small,
stuffy, none too clean; the beds little more comfortable
than the wagons. Besides, twenty-five cents! You got
twenty-five cents for half a barrel of tomatoes. You got
twenty-five cents for a sack of potatoes. Onions brought
seventy-five cents a sack. Cabbages went a hundred heads
for two dollars, and they were five-pound heads. . . . No;
one did not pay out twenty-five cents for the mere
privilege of sleeping in a bed.

from *A Long Hard Journey:*
The Story of the Pullman Porter

by Patricia and Frederick McKissack

Once the passengers were comfortably seated [on the train] and their bags were stored, the porter attended to special requests. He might be handing out newspapers, helping a mother with restless children, or pointing out geographic points of interest to first-time travelers or foreign visitors.

The Pullman porter's primary focus was the customer's welfare. He was instructed—and very often tested—to answer all calls promptly and courteously, no matter what time the calls were made.

When it was time to make the beds, the porter was expected to move with speed and agility. The company rule book was precise. According to Nathaniel Hall, a porter, the rule book specified "the proper handling of the linen closet—the proper method of folding and putting away clean linen and blankets, the correct way of stacking laundry bags and dirty, discarded bedding. A sheet, towel, or pillowcase once unfolded cannot be used again, although it may be spotless. Technically, it is dirty and must make a round trip to the laundry before it can reenter the service."

Porters were not allowed to make noise. "Noise was tabooed," reported Hall. "And even a soft knock on the top of the berth [was] forbidden. A porter must gently shake the curtains on the bedding from without."

22
Nonfiction

from *Sally Ride:*
America's First Woman in Space
by Carolyn Blacknall

With the excitement of launch behind them, the STS-7 crew settled down to a busy day. Every 90 minutes, *Challenger* completed an orbit of the earth. On the seventh orbit, the crew planned to launch the Anik-C satellite.

Anik-C was a Canadian communications satellite. It would relay voice, pictures, and information services throughout Canada. In the Inuit Indian language, *Anik* means *brother.*

As the seventh orbit drew near, the astronauts prepared to launch the satellite. Bob Crippen and Rick Hauck opened the orbiter's payload bay doors and slowly turned the shuttle to the correct position. Sally Ride and John Fabian could see into the 60-foot-long cargo bay through the two small windows in the back of the flight deck. Three satellites and two satellite boosters were stored there.

The boosters were needed to push Anik-C and the other communications satellite, Palapa-B, into a higher orbit. *Challenger*'s orbit was 160 miles above the earth. Both satellites had to fly at an altitude of 22,300 miles to stay above the same position on the earth.

Sally and John, floating weightless in the flight deck, started the booster rocket spinning. The commander and pilot checked *Challenger*'s movement with scientists and computers in Houston. When the shuttle was in position, Sally and John launched the satellite out of the shuttle's payload bay.

from "The Speckled Band"

by Arthur Conan Doyle

I had no keener pleasure than in following Holmes in his professional investigations, and in admiring the rapid deductions, as swift as intuitions, and yet always founded on a logical basis, with which he unraveled the problems which were submitted to him. I rapidly threw on my coat, and was ready in a few minutes to accompany my friend down to the sitting room. A lady dressed in black and heavily veiled, who had been sitting in the window, rose as we entered.

"Good morning, madam," said Holmes cheerily. "My name is Sherlock Holmes. This is my friend and associate, Dr. Watson, before whom you can speak as freely as before myself. Ha, I am glad to see that Mrs. Hudson has had the good sense to light the fire. Pray draw up to it, and I shall order you a cup of hot coffee, for I observe that you are shivering."

"It is not cold which makes me shiver," said the woman in a low voice, changing her seat as requested.

"What then?"

"It is fear, Mr. Holmes. It is terror." She raised her veil as she spoke, and we could see that she was indeed in a pitiable state of agitation, her face all drawn and gray, with restless, frightened eyes, like those of some hunted animal.

from "Appetizer"

by Robert H. Abel

I lay on the seat panting, curled like a child, shuddered when the bear slammed against the pickup's side. The bear pressed her nose to the window, then curiously, unceremoniously licked the glass with her tongue. I know (and you know) she could have shattered the glass with a single blow, and I tried to imagine what I should do if indeed she resorted to this simple expedient. Fisherman that I am, I had nothing in the cab of the truck to defend myself with except a tire iron, and that not readily accessible behind the seat I was cowering on. My best defense, obviously, was to start the pickup and drive away.

Just as I sat up to the steering wheel and inserted the key, however, Ms. Bear slammed her big paws onto the hood and hoisted herself aboard. The pickup shuddered with the weight of her, and suddenly the windshield was full of her golden fur. I beeped the horn loud and long numerous times, but this had about the same effect as my singing, only caused her to shake her huge head, which vibrated the truck terribly. She stomped around on the hood and then lay down, back against the windshield, which now appeared to have been covered by a huge shag rug.

25

from **"My Mother and Father"**

by Budge Wilson

I was born in Grace Maternity Hospital in Halifax, entering the world noisily and with confidence, to greet a mother who was already a widow. Far from her home in the south of France, she spent eight solitary days in the hospital, and then wrapped me in a blue blanket and took me home to an empty house.

It was early November when we entered that house, and France must have seemed a hundred light-years away. My mother had come to Nova Scotia as a young war bride in 1919, and after ten childless years had finally given birth to her first and last baby. The next several months of my life in that home must have been terrible indeed for her. She and my father had moved from Wolfville to Halifax shortly before he died, and she was therefore living in a strange city as well as in a foreign land. Although she had an almost perfect mastery of English, she retained a slight French accent, and was considered strange, alien, too exotic for safety. As a result, she had few acquaintances, no close friends, and of course no husband. Furthermore, it would be six months before one could expect any semblance of summer to soften Canada's stern, uncompromising East Coast.

from *Matilda*

by Roald Dahl

There was a muddy pond at the bottom of Lavender's garden and this was the home of a colony of newts. The newt, although fairly common in English ponds, is not often seen by ordinary people because it is a shy and murky creature. It is an incredibly ugly gruesome-looking animal, rather like a baby crocodile but with a shorter head. It is quite harmless but doesn't look it. It is about six inches long and very slimy, with a greenish-grey skin on top and an orange-colored belly underneath. It is, in fact, an amphibian, which can live in or out of water.

That evening Lavender went to the bottom of the garden determined to catch a newt. They are swiftly-moving animals and not easy to get hold of. She lay on the bank for a long time waiting patiently until she spotted a whopper. Then, using her school hat as a net, she swooped and caught it. She had lined her pencil-box with pond-weed ready to receive the creature, but she discovered that it was not easy to get the newt out of the hat and into the pencil-box. It wriggled and squirmed like quicksilver and, apart from that, the box was only just long enough to take it.

from *Snake's Daughter*

by Gail Hosking Gilberg

While many fathers went to Vietnam once, my father kept going back until he died there.

Once on one of his return trips home, he sat on the floor of our apartment wearing black Vietnamese pajamalike clothes, eating rice with chopsticks. While we ate meat loaf and mashed potatoes at the table, we listened to him speak about the men he left behind. I see now that the magical country of Vietnam had taken over his life, just like the war and the men at his side who became the reasons for fighting the war. Vietnam had a curious hold on my father I couldn't begin to understand then.

On another visit home, he went with me to a high school football game dressed in his full military dress uniform. I had spent my life seeing him in uniform, and I knew he took it seriously. His pants were tucked into his polished black boots and all his insignia were aligned in their proper places. But that night as he stood on the bleachers dressed differently from anyone else, surrounded by civilians, I began to feel uncomfortable. It confused me. Had I known the right words then, I would have asked what it was all about: the war, the uniform, his always going away.

Pronunciation Guide

insignia: in sig′ nē ə

from *Now Is Your Time!*
by Walter Dean Myers

Using the pen name Iola, [Ida B. Wells] began writing for a religious publication called *The Evening Star*. Her well-written, lively articles soon attracted the attention of another religious publication, a weekly called *The Living Way*.

It was common practice at the time for newspapers to "borrow" articles from one another. Soon the work published with Iola's by-line was being reprinted in a number of African-American newspapers. Ida accepted a part-time job as a regular correspondent, receiving the fancy salary of one dollar a week.

Ida Wells wanted justice for her people and for women. She wasn't willing to take life on anyone else's terms. Freedom, she felt, meant control of one's own life. She fought for that control at every opportunity. In 1889 she was invited to write for a small paper owned by two men in Memphis: *Free Speech and Headlight*. One of the men was the editor, and the other the sales manager. Ida would be the only woman and the only employee without a title. It didn't sound very much like equality to the young woman. With money she had saved, she insisted on buying a share of the paper so that she would be an equal to the men.

Nellie Bly: Exposing the Truth

In 1888, Joseph Pulitzer, owner of the famous newspaper *The World,* asked Nellie Bly to write an article. He wanted her to investigate rumors of cruelty and neglect in the New York City insane asylum. The only way for Nellie to learn the truth was to become a patient herself. That meant she had to pretend she was crazy.

After being admitted to the hospital, Nellie soon learned that the staff did not pay much attention to any of the patients. She had expected medical care at the hospital to be minimal, but she was not prepared for the kind of heartless treatment that she saw all around her. Nellie was equally stunned by the filthy living conditions that prevailed throughout the hospital.

After a couple of days in that inhumane environment, Nellie was ready to get out. When she tried to explain to a doctor that she was not sick, he simply laughed and walked away.

Eventually, however, with the help of Pulitzer, Nellie was freed, and she began to work on her story. When she finished, Pulitzer ran it on the front page of *The World.* The story instantly created a scandal, stirring the public's concern for the mentally ill. Nellie was delighted that her newspaper article helped to change the city's attitude toward the mentally ill.

from *Frankenstein*

by Mary Shelley

"One day, when I was oppressed by cold, I found a fire which had been left by some wandering beggars, and was overcome with delight at the warmth I experienced from it. In my joy I thrust my hand into the live embers, but quickly drew it out again with a cry of pain. How strange, I thought, that the same cause should produce such opposite effects! I examined the materials of the fire, and to my joy found it to be composed of wood. I quickly collected some branches; but they were wet, and would not burn. I was pained at this, and sat still watching the operation of the fire. The wet wood which I had placed near the heat dried, and itself became inflamed. I reflected on this; and, by touching the various branches, I discovered the cause, and busied myself in collecting a great quantity of wood, that I might dry it, and have a plentiful supply of fire. When night came on, and brought sleep with it, I was in the greatest fear lest my fire should be extinguished. I covered it carefully with dry wood and leaves, and placed wet branches upon it; and then, spreading my cloak, I lay on the ground, and sunk into sleep."

from *The Kidnapped Prince: The Life of Olaudah Equiano*

by Olaudah Equiano

adapted by Ann Cameron

In our village we were always ready for war. These wars were usually surprise attacks from strangers from another district who wanted to take prisoners or booty. Often, the attacks came when we were out of the village, working in the fields.

When we were afraid of the village being invaded, we guarded the streets leading to our houses with stakes struck into the ground. The exposed ends of the stakes had sharp points dipped in poison. The attacker who stepped on one would die.

It took a couple of hours to walk to our fields from the village. To prevent surprise attacks on the way to the fields, neighbors always walked together, carrying their hoes and axes and shovels—and their weapons too.

Our weapons were guns, bows and arrows, and broad two-edged swords. We also had spears, and also huge shields that could cover a man from head to foot.

Everybody was taught how to use these weapons, even the women. Our whole district was like a volunteer army. We all knew the warning signals, like the firing of a gun at night. When a signal came, we grabbed our weapons and rushed out of our houses to fight.

from **"Prime Time"**

by Henry Louis Gates Jr.

The simple truth is that the civil rights era came late to Piedmont, even though it came early to our television set. We could watch what was going on Elsewhere on television, but the marches and sit-ins were as remote to us as, in other ways, was the all-colored world of *Amos and Andy*—a world full of black lawyers, black judges, black nurses, black doctors.

Politics aside, though, we were starved for images of ourselves and searched TV to find them. Everybody, of course, watched sports, because Piedmont was a big sports town. Making the big leagues was like getting to Heaven, and everybody had hopes that they could, or a relative could. We'd watch the games day and night, and listen on radio to what we couldn't see. Everybody knew the latest scores, batting averages, rbi's, and stolen bases. Everybody knew the standings in the leagues, who could still win the pennant and how. Everybody liked the Dodgers because of Jackie Robinson, the same way everybody still voted Republican because of Abraham Lincoln. Sports on the mind, sports in the mind. The only thing to rival the Valley in fascination was the big-league baseball diamond.

from *Dolphin Man:*
Exploring the World of Dolphins

by Laurence Pringle

Suddenly dolphins rose to the surface in groups of two and three on both sides of the boat. For an instant each dolphin revealed the top of its head and body, including its big dorsal (back) fin, before diving under again. And in that instant Randy Wells began to call out their names:

"Pumpkin . . . Lightning . . . Merrily! And there's 55!"

In another half minute the dolphins rose to breathe again. "There's 75 and her calf, and Killer and her calf," Randy called. Soon he had identified four more dolphins for a total of a dozen—about a tenth of the bottlenose dolphins that live in Sarasota Bay on Florida's central western coast.

The boat followed the dolphins slowly as crew members took photographs of them and wrote down notes about their location and behavior. Randy and his crew discussed the identity of each dolphin, trying to make sure that they were correct.

The photographs they took were not casual snapshots. Each year the research team led by Randy Wells takes twenty thousand photos of dolphins to record marks on their dorsal fins and other distinctive features that are clues to their identification. Each year they also capture some of the dolphins in nets to briefly study them more closely, and to collect blood samples and other information before they release them.

from *Marie Curie*
by Angela Bull

[Pierre Curie] wanted the university simply to acknowledge the value of his work, and this they did not do. The French government, in 1902, actually offered him their highest decoration, the Legion of Honor, for his contribution to French science, but Pierre turned it down. "I do not feel the slightest need of being decorated," he wrote, "but I am in the greatest need of a laboratory." Still the academic world ignored him.

The Curies were always short of money. Marie had no salary or grant, and Pierre's salary was so low that it was quickly swallowed up by their living expenses, and by the wages of the maid and nurse, who looked after the house and little Irene. There was none to spare for advancing their research, and so, to earn a bit more, Marie took a job in a girls' school, where she taught physics two days a week. She was an excellent teacher, one of the first to allow her pupils to try practical experiments. More importantly, the work gave her a regular break from the contaminated atmosphere of the shed—something which Pierre never had. But Marie did not realize her good fortune. She only grumbled at the time she wasted in preparing her lessons, teaching, and traveling to and fro.

35 from "An Occurrence at Owl Creek Bridge"

Fiction

by Ambrose Bierce

By nightfall he was fatigued, footsore, famishing. The thought of his wife and children urged him on. At last he found a road which led him in what he knew to be the right direction. It was as wide and straight as a city street, yet it seemed untraveled. No fields bordered it, no dwelling anywhere. Not so much as the barking of a dog suggested human habitation. The black bodies of the trees formed a straight wall on both sides, terminating on the horizon in a point, like a diagram in a lesson in perspective. Overhead, as he looked up through this rift in the wood, shone great golden stars looking unfamiliar and grouped in strange constellations. He was sure they were arranged in some order which had a secret and malign significance. The wood on either side was full of singular noises, among which—once, twice, and again—he distinctly heard whispers in an unknown tongue.

His neck was in pain and lifting his hand to it he found it horribly swollen. He knew that it had a circle of black where the rope had bruised it. His eyes felt congested; he could no longer close them. His tongue was swollen with thirst.

Pronunciation Guide

malign: mə līn'

from *Charlotte Brontë and Jane Eyre*

by **Stewart Ross**

Patrick Brontë's duties as a clergyman kept him very busy. Even so, he always made time for his children. He ate breakfast and dinner with them. He guided their prayers and their reading—the whole family were great readers—and taught them history and geography. Whenever he could, he joined them for the high point of their day—lively romps over the sweeping moors.

The natural landscape made a deep impression on the young Charlotte. Many years later she wrote how Jane Eyre, fleeing from the deceitful human world, found peace in the "golden desert" of the "spreading moor." Nature was steadfast and true. To the orphan Jane it was a "universal mother" that loved her when the world did not. There were times when Charlotte, Jane's creator, must have felt the same.

Since all the Brontë children had powerful imaginations, there was never a dull moment when they played together. Their favorite indoor pursuits were making up games and stories and performing plays they had written. The central character was always the Duke of Wellington, Charlotte's hero, who had defeated Napoleon at Waterloo. If her brother or sisters ever suggested replacing the Duke with Napoleon or Julius Caesar, there would be an argument. Then Patrick would have to come out of his study to sort things out.

from *Robots Rising*
by Carol Sonenklar

Even though scientists can program a robot to do difficult tasks or even specific complex mathematics, they cannot make a robot walk upright, like a human—it's too hard. When you walk, you must continuously balance yourself to adjust to whatever bumps in the road or obstacles you encounter. Balancing is an exquisitely complicated ability: your brain must give out a steady stream of instructions to your nervous system and then to the muscles of your bones, and your vision, for starters.

In the mid-1980s, Rodney Brooks, a famous roboticist at MIT, noticed that insects and spiders, who don't have very large or complicated brains, could move over any terrain, find food for themselves, and hide from predators. Their six or eight legs gave them great stability and mobility; their antennae sensed obstacles and danger. But they did all this without a large central brain "telling" them what to do, so they didn't "learn" this behavior as we do.

And Brooks thought: Why not build a robot that has the brain of an insect?

So he did. In so doing, Brooks changed the way a lot of people think robots should be built. Six-legged *Genghis*, created in 1988 in Brooks's Mobot Laboratory at MIT, was the first walking insect robot. Instead of a central nervous system, his robot had various interconnected motion and light sensors located all over its body.

Pronunciation Guide

roboticist: rō bot′ i sist   Genghis: geng′ gis

from *Only Earth and Sky Last Forever*

by Nathaniel Benchley

When I got near the trap I led my pony into the woods and tethered him where he couldn't be seen from above. Then, working only by the light of the stars, I moved the last bits of sod and grass near the hole, took the pieces of jackrabbit out of my sack and put them on top of the covering, and then climbed into the hole. Lying on my back, I pulled the sod in place over my head, getting my eyes and mouth full of dirt as I did. . . .

I lay on my back, silently praying for the strength I was going to need, and I slowly became aware of the coming of day. Little chinks of gray showed through the covering over my head, then the gray turned to blue, and the blue to bright white. I could see small patches of sky, which was a help, and I only hoped that any eagle up there wouldn't be able to see me as well. Time passed, and as the sun began to warm the ground I could smell the jackrabbit, even through the turf and grass. I wondered if it would attract a coyote or a wolf, and figured I'd have to take care of that situation if and when it happened.

from *Drifting Snow: An Arctic Search*

by James Houston

There was no landing strip on Nesak, a rough, rocky island named with the Inuit word meaning "hat" because the island was shaped just like a hat.

The four families dwelling above the beach continued to live their nomadic lives in spite of modern times. They moved with every season, following the animals—birds, fish, and caribou—animals that supported them and allowed them to stay alive. In winter and in early spring, these hunting families lived on this island. Later, they would pull their boats on sleds behind their snowmobiles across the great expanse of sea ice to the mouth of the Kokjuak River on Baffin Island. It would be a long day's journey for them, but the plane had taken only a few minutes to cross.

Inside their winter tent, Poota pulled on his silver-spotted, knee-length, outer sealskin pants, and then his best navy-blue parka with red-and-white braid near his hips and around his wrists. Setting his many-colored woolen hat upon his head, then pulling up his hood, he hurried through the tent's low door. Any day when they had visitors was a very special day.

As the strong metal skis of the bright red plane touched down on the snow, he watched the plane bounce, then hop, then skim roughly over the hard white drifts.

Pronunciation Guide

Nesak: nē' sak
Kokjuak: kō' kōōak

Inuit: i' nōō wət

from *Tales from Watership Down*
by Richard Adams

The Down lay empty all around, and the breeze brought no scent of [enemies] but only the familiar smells of juniper and thyme. After the days of restriction in the frost-bound burrows, the spaciousness was exhilarating, and several of the rabbits began leaping and chasing one another almost like hares. Hazel felt the release as fully as anyone and joined happily in a mock fight with Speedwell and Silver in and out of the junipers. Running away from Speedwell, he ran down the steep north-facing slope, pulled up sharply in front of a thornbush and lost his balance, rolling over against a sodden tussock.

Picking himself up, Hazel, with a shock, saw a dog racing uphill toward him, yapping with excitement. It was a smooth-haired fox terrier, white with brown patches, soaking wet and muddy from the ditches and furrows down below. Hazel turned, breaking into his limping run, but even as he put on his best speed he knew that he was not fast enough; the dog was gaining on him. Desperately he changed direction, dodging one way and another, and as he did he felt the dog's breath panting closer, almost on top of him.

Pronunciation Guide

thyme: tīm   tussock: tus' ək

from "The Golden Darters"

by Elizabeth Winthrop

———————————— ∞∞∞ ————————————

I was twelve years old when my father started tying flies. It was an odd habit for a man who had just undergone a serious operation on his upper back, but, as he remarked to my mother one night, at least it gave him a world over which he had some control.

The family grew used to seeing him hunched down close to his tying vise, hackle pliers in one hand, thread bobbin in the other. We began to bandy about strange phrases—foxy quills, bodkins, peacock hurl. Father's corner of the living room was off limits to the maid with the voracious and destructive vacuum cleaner. Who knew what precious bit of calf's tail or rabbit fur would be sucked away never to be seen again.

Because of my father's illness, we had gone up to our summer cottage on the lake in New Hampshire a month early. None of my gang of friends ever came till the end of July, so in the beginning of that summer I hung around home watching my father as he fussed with the flies. I was the only child he allowed to stand near him while he worked.

Pronunciation Guide

voracious: vō rā' shəs

from *The Moon of the Alligators*

by Jean Craighead George

Two eyes poked above the still water. Each iris was silver-yellow and each pupil black and narrow. They were the eyes of the alligator of Sawgrass Hole, who was floating like a log on the surface of the water as she watched for food. She saw the blue sky above her, and because her eyes were on the top and to the rear of her head, she saw all the way behind her to the tall cypress trees. Their limbs spread like silver wires above a tangle of sweet bay and buttonbushes.

The alligator did not move, but watched and waited even though hunger gnawed her belly. She had eaten little since June, when the rainy season had flooded her home and the prey she fed upon had swum away. Now her sense of seasonal rhythm told her that the afternoon's cloudless sky meant the end of the rains and hurricanes, and the return of the wildlife to her water hole. The moon of October was the beginning of southern Florida's dry season. The water level would fall. The fish, frogs, turtles, and birds would come back to Sawgrass Hole, where she lived. They would be followed by the herons and ibis, egrets, . . . [and] water turkeys, and she would eat well once more.

Pronunciation Guide

ibis: ī′ bis   egrets: ē′ grits

43

Fiction

from *The Samurai and the Long-Nosed Devils*

by Lensey Namioka

Breathless after crossing the mountain pass, the two travelers stood for a moment and looked down on the dark gray roofs of Miyako. The capital city was situated in a small plain surrounded on three sides by mountains. On this July afternoon, the heat lay trapped in the city as if in a large bowl. The air vibrated with the heat, and to the tired eyes of the travelers, the roof tiles seemed to be jumping up and down.

The men each wore two swords thrust into their sashes, marking them as samurai. Their kimonos were of silk and had once been even elegant, but they were now torn and white with dust. On their feet the travelers wore straw sandals nearly falling apart from hard use. Still, the two men carried themselves with the unconscious haughtiness of the warrior class, although it was clear from their shabby condition that they were *ronin,* or unemployed samurai.

As they made their way down into the city, Matsuzo, the younger of the two ronin, removed his large basket-shaped hat and wiped his face with his sleeve. "How much money do we have left?" he asked.

Zenta, his companion, groped inside the front of his kimono and brought out a few coins. "I'm afraid this is all we have."

Matsuzo's face fell. "Well, it should be enough for a bath, at least."

Pronunciation Guide

samurai: sam' o͞o rī

The Development of Ballet

Ballet began in the royal courts during the Renaissance. At that time it became common for kings and queens, as well as other nobility, to participate in pageants that included music, poetry, and dance. As these entertainments moved from the Italian courts to the French ones, court ladies began participating in them. Though their long dresses prevented much movement, they were able to perform elaborate walking patterns. It was not until the 1600s that women dancers shortened their skirts, changed to flat shoes, and began doing some of the leaps and turns performed by men.

It was also in the 1600s that professional ballet began. The five basic foot positions from which all ballet steps begin were finalized. In the late 1700s another important change occurred. Ballet began to tell a story on its own. By the early 1800s dancers learned to rise on their toes to make it appear that they were floating.

Classical ballet as we know it today was influenced primarily by Russian dancing. One of the most influential figures of the early 20th century was Sergei Diaghilev. His dance company brought a new energy and excitement to ballet. One of his chief assistants, George Balanchine, went on to found the New York City Ballet in 1948 and to influence new generations of dancers.

Pronunciation Guide

Diaghilev: dyä′ gi lef′   Balanchine: bal′ ən chēn′

45

Nonfiction

from *To the Top of the World: Adventures with Arctic Wolves*

by Jim Brandenburg

Wolves are probably one of the most social animals outside of the primates. The success of the pack depends strongly on a highly developed system of communication with neighboring packs as well as between individual pack members. Smell, vision, and hearing play crucial roles in such communication.

The most well-known form of communication wolves use is their howl. Howling begins at a very early age. Within weeks after emerging from the den, the pups [turn] their tiny snouts to the sky right alongside their parents.

I was often able to watch and listen to a songfest by the whole pack. Each had his or her distinctive voice and a preferred range of notes. [A wolf I called] Midback, for instance, had a high-pitched, almost whiny cry, whereas Left Shoulder would howl in the lower octaves.

Whatever their preferred notes, however, one thing was certain. Every wolf avoided hitting the same note as any of its packmates. When this happened by accident, one of the voices would frantically shuffle about until discord could be achieved once again. This phenomenon apparently has evolved to suit the scattered distribution of the Arctic wolves across an unfriendly environment, not always in safe numbers. With as many different tones as possible in its howling, a pack can give the impression of greater size and can intimidate possible intruders.

46

Fiction

from *Hidden Trail*
by Jim Kjelgaard

He turned south, toward the big bend of the river, [his dog] Buckles scouting along first on one side of him, then the other.

As he approached the bend, motion on the river brought him to a sudden stop.

Four or five hundred yards away, eleven great gray wolves trotted across the frozen river, emerged from the willows on the far side, and continued at right angles to the southward direction in which Jase was traveling. They knew he was there and Jase knew they knew, but they did not hurry. They seemed to sense that the human and dog were too far away to be any threat.

Jase took out his camera, focused his telephoto lens on the lazily traveling pack, and shot a sequence. He knew even before he started shooting that he would not get a good sequence under the hazy light conditions, but that was unimportant. He wanted it for the record, for he was certain that the pack had come into the valley of the Mary to prey on the wintering elk.

As he sheathed his camera again, Jase became aware that there had been a shift in the wind direction. For three days it had blown out of the north, but now it was coming from the east, and was definitely warmer. He glanced up at the sky.

from *Mary Cassatt:*
Portrait of an American Impressionist
by Tom Streissguth

While still in school, Mary [Cassatt] decided that she would make a living on her own as a painter. After graduating from high school, she had to spend a long time working up enough courage to break the news to her father. She would have to choose the right words and find him in the right mood. She knew he might not take it very well.

She would have to return to Europe. To learn to paint, that was where one must study, and the best way to study was to copy museum pictures and work in artists' studios in France, Spain, or Italy. She would learn from professional artists and meet other students. She would travel. Europe wasn't like Philadelphia; there were beautiful sculptures in the streets and squares. There were paintings displayed in the windows of small galleries and on the walls of vast cathedrals. People in Europe had art surrounding them—they talked about art like Americans talked about money!

Robert Cassatt was patient and understanding. He listened to his daughter. He knew that Mary had talent, but even so, talented young ladies should not be bothered with careers. They especially did not work as painters. Art could be a hobby they might try, but only when their real duties, as wives and as mothers, allowed them time.

48

Fiction

from *Taking Sides*

by Gary Soto

When he had arrived in the new neighborhood, Lincoln had liked the peacefulness of sprinklers hissing on green lawns and the sycamores that lined the street. He liked the splashes of flowers and neatly piled firewood. He liked the hedges where jays built scrawny nests and bickered when cats slithered too close. The people seemed distant, but that was fine with him. It was better than the loud cars that raced up and down his old block. It was better than littered streets and graffiti-covered walls. . . .

Now, three months later, Lincoln was having second thoughts. He missed his old school and its mural of brown, black, and yellow kids linking arms in friendship. He had liked Franklin Junior High, tough as it was, with its fights in the hallways and in the noisy cafeteria. He had liked to walk among brown faces and stand with the Vietnamese and Korean kids. He missed his friends, especially his number-one man, Tony Contreras, whom he had known forever, even before first grade when Tony accidentally knocked out Lincoln's front baby teeth going down the slide. And he missed Vicky. They had parted on bad terms, but Lincoln felt that if he could speak with her everything would turn out OK.

from *April and the Dragon Lady*
by Lensey Namioka

When I came home from school on Monday and opened the front door, a cloud of delectable smells hit me in the face.

These days Grandma still insisted on doing most of the cooking, but she prepared simple meals—rice and a couple of stir-fried dishes of meat and vegetables. On weekends I took her to Chinatown and stocked up on a variety of Chinese convenience foods like sausages, pickled eggs, cans of vegetables already sliced and cooked, and packages of frozen steamed breads and savory pastries.

But the smells today were a sign of a major cooking effort. I was immediately worried that Grandma might be working too hard. However energetic, she was after all seventy years old. In China, seventy-year-old women were supported on both sides when they got up and tottered around, especially in the old days when they had bound feet.

There was something unfamiliar, too, about the combination of spices. Was she trying out a new dish? I could smell star anise, Sichuan pickle, and sesame oil. I had to swallow hard, because I was literally drooling.

After putting my backpack down, I turned to the living room and found a little boy there sitting on the couch, watching television.

Pronunciation Guide

anise: an' is   Sichuan: si' chwän

from *Isaac Bashevis Singer:*
The Life of a Storyteller
by Lila Perl

There were both bad and good aspects to Isaac's job as a proofreader. The work, as he'd expected, was monotonous, hard on the eyes, and sometimes exasperating. The writers who contributed to *Literary Pages* often handed in material that was not quite ready to be set in print. It was Isaac's job to check through the Yiddish printers' proofs for errors and to correct them. The stories themselves, Isaac often felt, were poorly conceived and written, and he wondered why the editors bought them. Isaac harbored dreams of producing some publishable writing of his own. His head buzzed with ideas, but who would ever buy a story from him?

Though Isaac's days were now mainly full of toil and poverty, there *were* several advantages to living on his own as a young man in Warsaw. Being away from his family and having given up his religious studies, Isaac ceased to dress as a religious Jew. Gone were his earlocks and his Hasidic garments, for he now led a worldly life. As an employee of a literary journal, Isaac was admitted to the Warsaw Writers' Club, and this became for him the closest thing to a home. At the Writers' Club, one could find a warm corner in winter in which to sit and read, do some writing, or play chess.

Pronunciation Guide

Hasidic: hə sid' ik

The Seneca Falls Convention

In 1848 Seneca Falls, located in upstate New York, was a rural town. In July, a notice in the local newspaper announced that public meetings would be held in the local chapel on the subject of women's rights. Only a few dozen people were expected to attend. To the astonishment of the organizers, hundreds of women showed up.

One of the meetings' organizers was Elizabeth Cady Stanton. As she rose to speak, she did not know how well she would present her ideas. She had never spoken in public before.

She read from the Declaration of Sentiments and Resolutions, a document in which several complaints and demands were presented regarding the rights of women. One demand was for the right to vote.

"'Resolved,'" Stanton read, "'that it is the duty of the women of this country to secure to themselves their sacred right to the elective franchise.'"

As expected, there was opposition to the resolution. Guided by Stanton, the resolution finally passed—by a narrow margin.

The public reacted to the resolution with outrage. Newspaper editorials accused the women of trying to tear down the nation. One paper accused them of trying to upset "existing institutions and [seeking to] overturn all the social relations of life."

Despite the outcry, important changes had been set in motion.

from *No Promises in the Wind*

by Irene Hunt

I stared at the faded paper on the wall in front of me without really seeing it until I became conscious of the yellowed figures of cowboys riding their broncs in precise paths from baseboard to ceiling. My mother had allowed me to select that paper five years before when I was no older than [my younger brother] Joey, and I had held out for cowboys and broncs, scorning Mom's preference for pots of flowers or bright colored birds. I studied the horses and their daredevil riders for a long time as if they mattered. They didn't, of course, but concentrating on them kept me awake.

Finally I [fully awakened]. My paper route didn't mean much money, but it was important. Dad had been out of work for eight months, and only the day before, my sister had received notice of a cut-back in personnel which cost her the clerking job she'd had for nearly a year. Every few pennies counted in our family; a job was a job, and to risk losing it by being late was out of the question.

It was dark in the kitchen when I went downstairs, but I could see the outline of my mother's figure as she stood at the stove.

from *Thomas Edison:*
American Inventor

by Roselyn and Ray Eldon Hiebert

Acrid smells frequently poured out of the basement workshop as Tom [Edison] plunged into the world of chemistry. The cellar became littered with the remains of chemicals and bottles, and his parents grew concerned that something serious might happen. Finally his mother told him to clean up the laboratory and quit his experiments, but the boy was so grief-stricken that she relented. She made a rigid rule, however, that he must lock the cellar when he was not working, so that nobody could get in and cause an accident.

For hours, Tom locked himself in the dark room beneath the house, puttering with batteries and chemical formulas instead of playing outdoors. When his mother called him for his tutoring, he worked with her on other studies, but he never did well in English composition. Even later, when he was nineteen, his letters home showed a sad lack of proficiency in writing.

Tom's mother understood how he loved to experiment and she sometimes let him work throughout the day with his wires, test tubes, and gases.

"My mother was the making of me," Edison later said. "She understood me. She let me follow my bent."

from *Buried Onions*
by Gary Soto

He walked over to the hill and stood on it, his shadow like a flagpole behind him. He threw back his head as he drained his coffee and then jumped up and down, smiling, puffs of dirt rising around his work boots. I knew he was imagining how his yard would bloom and his neighbors would stop to admire it. In mid-May it was a nice dream.

"I'm going to plant a birch," he said as he climbed down.

I asked him about the tree, and he said it was the kind of tree that grows in New England, especially along the shady twists and turns of babbling brooks. I couldn't imagine such a place. I couldn't imagine a place where the sun didn't gnaw at my eyes, gnaw with its bright hunger so that every other minute my pupils had to adjust themselves. I closed my eyes for a brief second and wondered what this tree was doing in Fresno. No rivers spun through our town, and it certainly didn't look like New England, though we did have one barren subdivision called Connecticut Meadows. I had to laugh at that because most of the people who lived there were Korean.

Mr. Stiles said to dig where he'd been standing.

from *Petrouchka: The Story of the Ballet*

retold by Vivian Werner

It was Shrove Tuesday, the day of the annual Shrovetide Fair, and the people of old St. Petersburg were in a festive mood. They gathered in the town square, laughing and joking, waving and shouting greetings to one another, slapping one another on the back.

They all knew that Lent would begin the very next day. There would be no feasting after that—no dancing, no merrymaking at all until Easter, many long weeks away.

Snow floated down in feathery flakes on that Shrove Tuesday, over a hundred and fifty years ago. It settled alike on the kerchiefed heads of peasant women and the elegant coats of gentlemen. It drifted over the graceful yellow and pink and pale blue buildings that ringed the square, and coated the colorfully decorated booths inside it.

Early as it was, those scarlet and green and gold booths had been set up even earlier. Now the old women bustled about, busily setting out their wares. Shivering, they pulled their fringed shawls closer around their shoulders to ward off the cold.

One pudgy little woman in a long, bright apron festooned her booth with fat ropes of sausage. Another polished the big brass samovar in which she would brew her fragrant tea.

Pronunciation Guide

samovar: sam′ ə vär′

"I Will Fight No More Forever"

For centuries the Nez Perce had called Oregon's Wallowa Valley home. However, by 1877 the U.S. government had ordered the Nez Perce to move to a reservation in Idaho. Chief Joseph resisted but finally, to protect the lives of his people, he began leading them toward the Idaho reservation. Along the way, some of his men rebelled and killed a group of settlers. Chief Joseph knew the Army would retaliate, and so he changed course, seeking the safety of Canada.

For months, the outnumbered Nez Perce warriors evaded or fought the Army troops that pursued them. Finally, the Army caught the group by surprise, surrounding them. After five days Chief Joseph surrendered. The Nez Perce had traveled over one thousand miles and were about forty miles from their destination.

At the surrender Chief Joseph gave a now-famous speech that includes these words: "The little children are freezing to death. My people, some of them, have run away to the hills and have no blankets, no food. No one knows where they are—perhaps freezing to death. I want to have time to look for my children and see how many I can find. Maybe I shall find them among the dead. Hear me, my chiefs. I am tired; my heart is sick and sad. From where the sun now stands, I will fight no more forever."

Pronunciation Guide

Nez Perce: nez' pûrs'

from **"Brother Death"**

by Sherwood Anderson

There was a back porch to the Grey house . . . and from the porch steps a path led down to a stone springhouse. A spring came out of the ground just there, and there was a tiny stream that went along the edge of a field, past two large barns and out across a meadow to a creek—called a "branch" in Virginia, and the two trees stood close together beyond the springhouse and the fence.

They were [strong] trees, their roots down in the rich, always damp soil, and one of them had a great limb that came down near the ground, so that Ted and Mary could climb into it and out another limb into its brother tree, and in the fall, when other trees, at the front and side of the house, had shed their leaves, blood-red leaves still clung to the two oaks. They were like dry blood on gray days, but on other days, when the sun came out, the trees flamed against distant hills. The leaves clung, whispering and talking when the wind blew, so that the trees themselves seemed carrying on a conversation.

John Grey had decided he would have the trees cut. At first it was not a very definite decision. "I think I'll have them cut," he announced.

"But why?" his wife asked.

from *Into the Deep Forest with Henry David Thoreau*

Nonfiction

by Jim Murphy

"I think that I cannot preserve my health and spirits," Henry David Thoreau wrote in his journal, "unless I spend four hours a day . . . sauntering through the woods and over the hills and fields, absolutely free from all worldly engagements."

And so, every day for over thirty years, Henry would leave his home in Concord, Massachusetts, and stride through the surrounding swamps and brush and forest. It was only when he was away from town and the prying eyes of his neighbors that Henry felt truly free—to follow any path he chose, to study carefully what was around him, and to think any thought he wanted.

Few people meeting Henry for the first time would take him for much of a thinker. He liked to wear simple work shirts, rumpled pants, and boots that were heavily greased to keep water out. What is more, his hands were rough from years of hard work, while constant exposure to sun, rain, and icy winds had left his face tanned and deeply lined. But if his appearance was unremarkable, his mind was not. In fact, Henry David Thoreau is now considered one of the great American writers, philosophers, and naturalists of the nineteenth century.

from *On the Brink of Extinction: The California Condor*

by Caroline Arnold

A group of scientists watched anxiously as AC-9, the last of the free-flying California condors, circled overhead. Gliding gracefully on giant wings, the huge bird eyed the fresh carcass that lay in the clearing. Like other vultures, it depended on finding dead animals for its food. Finally AC-9 landed and cautiously approached the meat. Before the bird had time to escape, the scientists released their net and caught it. One person rushed forward to grab the condor and safely untangle it while another brought over a small carrier in which they would transport the bird to the zoo. AC-9 and the twenty-six other condors already in captivity were the only California condors left in the world. If they died, their species would become extinct. The scientists hoped that placing these birds together in male-female pairs would lead to successful breeding in zoos. After a few years, young condors could be returned to the wild to begin a new healthy flock.

For forty thousand years or more, California condors ranged across much of North America. They fed on the carcasses of giant sloths, mastodons, and other large mammals that roamed the continent during the last Ice Age. When these animals became extinct about ten thousand years ago, the condors disappeared everywhere except along the west coast.

from *My Daniel*
by Pam Conrad

I thought it was fun in those days to see Pa strapped to a plow like a horse, a workhorse that plodded along wordlessly while Ma steered the plow through the hard soil. I was too little to understand how poor we were.

I remember how everything was so slow and thick— the air, the sky, the dirt; Daniel's job was to plant the seeds. I followed along beside him through the heavy clods of dirt and watched as he dropped one seed after another before each of his bare feet. Daniel carried a sack full of seeds on his shoulder, and it seems I can remember him pulling a dry twig or flower out of the sack and tossing it at me with a big grin. The grin. I search my memories for the exact slant of his smile.

And then suddenly Daniel dropped to his knees in the soil. I crouched next to him, my hand on his knee, and watched as he pulled rocks from the dirt. The rocks were the size of the palm of my hand, and there—hundreds and hundreds of miles from any seashore—he had licked his fingers and, darkening the surfaces of the rocks, brought life to the delicate designs of clams and tiny seashells.

"Look, Julie," he had said, holding it out to me.

from *Survival: Earthquake*

by K. Duey and K. A. Bale

Fiction

It was almost dawn. Brendan O'Connor gripped the reins, struggling to control the nervous mare without slowing her down. Up and down Market Street wagon wheels gritted over the cobblestones. Drivers were hauling produce, laundry, milk, everything the hotels and restaurants would need for the day's business.

Brendan had worked hard to get this route and he wasn't going to lose it. His boss had the kind of temper no one wanted to set off. Two things made old man Hansen furious: losing money and late deliveries. Fancy San Francisco hotels like the Baldwin and the Palace would find another bakery if their wealthy guests had to wait for their fresh-baked bread and pastries.

The street lamps had been turned off a few minutes before and the city was enveloped by a deep blue predawn glow. Brendan shivered. The damp early morning chill seeped through his worn woolen jacket. He looked up at the fading crescent moon. There wasn't a cloud in the sky. Maybe it would be warmer today. Still, he needed to find a better blanket for his cot soon.

So far, no one had objected to his sleeping in a corner of the furniture warehouse.

62

from "Pizza in Warsaw, Torte in Prague"

by Slavenka Drakulić

Right after the overthrow of the Ceausescu government in Romania in December 1989, I read a report in the newspaper about life in Bucharest. There was a story about a man who ate the first banana in his life. He was an older man, a worker, and he said to a reporter shyly that he ate a whole banana, together with the skin, because he didn't know that he had to peel it. At first, I was moved by the isolation this man was forced to live in, by the fact that he never read or even heard what to do with a banana. But then something else caught my attention: *"It tasted good,"* he said. I can imagine this man, holding a sweet-smelling, ripe banana in his hand, curious and excited by it, as by a forbidden fruit. He holds it for a moment, then bites. It tastes strange but "good." It must have been good, even together with a bitter, tough skin, because it was something unachievable, an object of desire. It was not a banana that he was eating, but the promise, the hope of the future. So, he liked it no matter what its taste.

Pronunciation Guide

Ceausescu: cha͞o shes' k͞oo

from "President Cleveland, Where Are You?"

Fiction

by Robert Cormier

That was the autumn of the cowboy cards—Buck
Jones and Tom Tyler and Hoot Gibson and especially Ken
Maynard. The cards were available in those five-cent
packages of gum: pink sticks, three together, covered with
a sweet white powder. You couldn't blow bubbles with
that particular gum, but it couldn't have mattered less.
The cowboy cards were important—the pictures of those
rock-faced men with eyes of blue steel.

On those wind-swept, leaf-tumbling afternoons we
gathered after school on the sidewalk in front of Lemire's
Drugstore, across from St. Jude's Parochial School, and we
swapped and bargained and matched for the cards.
Because a Ken Maynard serial was playing at the Globe
every Saturday afternoon, he was the most popular
cowboy of all, and one of his cards was worth at least ten
of any other kind. Rollie Tremaine had a treasure of thirty
or so, and he guarded them jealously. He'd match you for
the other cards, but he risked his Ken Maynards only
when the other kids threatened to leave him out of the
competition altogether.

You could almost hate Rollie Tremaine. In the first
place, he was the only son of Auguste Tremaine, who
operated the Uptown Dry Goods Store, and he did not
live in a tenement.

64

Fiction

from *Horns of Plenty*

by Jane and Paul Annixter

The eagle screamed and the ram felt the impact of the human gaze, and threat again. The man did not reach for the gun; even if he had [the ram] Big Eye knew instinctively that the distance between was too great for danger. So he held his ground and crossed gazes with the man as if in challenge, while his hyper-awareness, born of his leadership, expanded and grew.

For the old ram each rising of the sun, each change of weather or shift of wind called for new strategy. Each day brought fresh problems to be solved. These he must always sense in advance, for with his band his authority was absolute, based as it was upon the primal law of the strongest, wisest and most courageous. His was a total responsibility, for where he led the band would follow. If he chose to go down the sheer face of a precipice where the only way was a series of leaps and balancings from one nubbin of rock to another and thence to an almost non-existent ledge, the flock would unhesitatingly follow. If in crises he were to leap to his death in some sheer abyss, there, too, the flock would go.

Pronunciation Guide

precipice: **pres′ ə pis**   abyss: **ə bis′**

from *The Lost Dispatch:* *A Story of Antietam*

by Donald J. Sobol

A mile raced by, and then another. With every passing second Wade expected to hear the shrill whine of a bullet reaching for him. Farther and farther from the Union camps he sped, body cramped low and cheek laid by [his horse] Outcast's plunging neck. But no rifle blast pierced the clenching stillness, no bullet singled him out. Night rested softly upon a land seemingly asleep and harmless.

At length he shifted up into the saddle and stole a rearward glance. The road behind lay straight for several hundred yards, and empty. He slowed Outcast to a trot, musing indignantly. . . . Mysterious sharpshooter—in a pig's ear!

Believing himself absolutely safe, he remained seated upright in the saddle. After crossing the James River on an old flatboat, he headed due west for Kentucky. A spring rain began to fall, and he dismounted to unstrap the slicker.

As his weight dropped upon one foot, the realization of why he had ridden this far unscathed darted through his mind.

A skilled marksman makes sure of his first shot, or does not shoot. Darkness and now rain made a galloping target too difficult to bring down. Far from being a daydream, Three-Fingers might well be all too real—a marksman who was biding his time and picking his spot.

from *Adventures in Courage*
by Dennis Brennan

The development of the dirigible marked the final phase of the history of the balloon. These gigantic airships became a popular means of air transportation. They could carry passengers great distances, even across oceans.

On May 3, 1937, a tragic accident climaxed the story of the dirigible. On that day a giant airship named the *Hindenburg* exploded while landing at Lakehurst, New Jersey, at the end of a transoceanic trip from Germany. Thirty-six of the 97 passengers aboard were killed and many more were horribly burned. This tragedy brought the era of the balloon to its end. Although dirigibles still are occasionally seen in the skies, their use has become very limited.

But even during the nineteenth century, many believed the balloon was not the final answer to man's desire for equality with the birds. They believed the true future of aviation lay in flight with winged aircraft, not with bulky, gas-filled bags.

Balloons flew because the gas inside them was lighter than the air. But birds are heavier than air, reasoned the men of the sky, and *they* fly.

How?

That was the question. How?

Is it not possible, they asked themselves, for man to construct a machine that would duplicate birds' flight?

Yes, they answered. It *is* possible.

Pronunciation Guide

dirigible: dir′ ə jə bəl

from "Sweet Potato Pie"

by Eugenia Collier

From up here on the fourteenth floor, my brother Charley looks like an insect scurrying among other insects. A deep feeling of love surges through me. Despite the distance, he seems to feel it, for he turns and scans the upper windows, but failing to find me, continues on his way.

I watch him moving quickly—gingerly, it seems to me—down Fifth Avenue and around the corner to his shabby taxicab. In a moment he will be heading back uptown.

I turn from the window and flop down on the bed, shoes and all. Perhaps because of what happened this afternoon or maybe just because I see Charley so seldom, my thoughts hover over him like hummingbirds. The cheerful, impersonal tidiness of this room is a world away from Charley's walk-up flat in Harlem and a hundred worlds from the bare, noisy shanty where he and the rest of us spent what there was of childhood. I close my eyes, and side by side I see the Charley of my boyhood and the Charley of this afternoon, as clearly as if I were looking at a split TV screen. Another surge of love, seasoned with gratitude, wells up in me.

from "A Walk to the Jetty"

by Jamaica Kincaid

When my father's stomach started to go bad, the doctor had recommended a walk every evening right after he ate his dinner. Sometimes he would take me with him. When he took me with him, we usually went to the jetty, and there he would sit and talk to the night watchman about cricket or some other thing that didn't interest me, because it was not personal; they didn't talk about their wives, or their children, or their parents, or about any of their likes and dislikes. They talked about things in such a strange way, and I didn't see what they found funny, but sometimes they made each other laugh so much that their guffaws would bound out to sea and send back an echo. I was always sorry when we got to the jetty and saw that the night watchman on duty was the one he enjoyed speaking to; it was like being locked up in a book filled with numbers and diagrams and what-ifs. For the thing about not being able to understand and enjoy what they were saying was I had nothing to take my mind off my fear of slipping in between the boards of the jetty.

from *My Year*

by Roald Dahl

No cuckoo has ever bothered to build its own nest or hatch or feed its young. The female (carrying her egg in her beak) searches the hedgerows until she finds the nest of another bird that already has eggs in it, and she slips her own egg in with the others and flies away and forgets all about it.

Usually, for some unknown reason, cuckoos choose a hedge sparrow's nest. . . . The extraordinary thing is that the mother hedge sparrow, when she returns and finds this dirty brown egg lying in her nest among her own blue beauties, does not seem to mind at all and proceeds to sit on it and incubate it together with her own.

Little does she know what is going to happen when all the eggs hatch. There will usually be four or five of her own eggs plus the one cuckoo's egg and when the baby chicks hatch out, the mother and father both feed them all, including the horrid cuckoo chick. Don't forget that the adult cuckoo is a bird three times as big as the hedge sparrow, and therefore the cuckoo chick grows three times as fast as the little sparrows. Then comes the slaughter. The overgrown baby cuckoo proceeds quite literally to push the baby hedge sparrows one by one out of the nest to die.

from *The Road from Coorain*
by Jill Ker Conway

Before being formally enrolled, I was taken for an interview with Miss Everett, the headmistress. To me she seemed like a benevolent being from another planet. She was over six feet tall, with the carriage and gait of a splendid athlete. Her dress was new to me. She wore a tweed suit of soft colors and battered elegance. She spoke in the plummy tones of a woman educated in England, and her intelligent face beamed with humor and curiosity. When she spoke, the habit of long years of teaching French made her articulate her words clearly and so forcefully that the unwary who stood too close were in danger of being sprayed like the audience too close to the footlights of a vaudeville show. "She looks strapping," she cheerfully commented to my mother, after talking to me for a few minutes alone. "She can begin tomorrow." Thereafter, no matter how I misbehaved, or what events brought me into her presence, I felt real benevolence radiating from Miss Everett.

The sight of her upright figure, forever striding across the school grounds, automatically caused her charges to straighten their backs. Those who slouched were often startled to have her appear suddenly behind them and seize their shoulders to correct their posture.

from *The Incredible Journey*

by Sheila Burnford

The late afternoon sun slanted through the branches overhead, and it looked invitingly snug and secure. The old dog stood for a minute, his heavy head hanging, and his tired body swaying slightly, then lay down on his side in the hollow. The cat, after a good deal of wary observation, made a little hollow among the spruce needles and curled around in it, purring softly. The young dog disappeared into the undergrowth and reappeared presently, his smooth coat dripping water, to lie down a little away apart from the others.

The old dog continued to pant exhaustedly for a long time, one hind leg shaking badly, until his eyes closed at last, the labored breaths came further and further apart, and he was sleeping—still, save for an occasional long shudder.

Later on, when darkness fell, the young dog moved over and stretched out closely at his side and the cat stalked over to lie between his paws; and so, warmed and comforted by their closeness, the old dog slept, momentarily unconscious of his aching, tired body or his hunger.

In the nearby hills a timber wolf howled mournfully; owls called and answered and glided silently by with great outspread wings; and there were faint whispers of movement and small rustling noises around all through the night.

72

from *My Own Two Feet*
by Beverly Cleary

The three of us, Mother, Dad, and I, stood on the sidewalk outside the Greyhound bus station in Portland, Oregon, searching for words we could not find or holding back words we could not speak. The sun, bronze from the smoke of September forest fires, cast an illusory light. Nothing seemed real, but it was. I was leaving, actually leaving, for California, the Golden State, land of poppies, big red geraniums, trees heavy with oranges, palm trees beneath cloudless skies, and best of all, no Depression. I had seen it all on postcards and in the movies, and so had the rest of my class at Grant High School. California was the goal of many. John Steinbeck had not yet, in 1934, revised our thinking.

And now I was one of the lucky ones going to this glorious place where people made movies all day and danced the night away. I was escaping the clatter of typewriters in business school and going instead to college. As I stood there in the smoky light in my neat navy blue dress, which Mother had measured a fashionable twelve inches from the floor when I made it, and with a five-dollar bill given to me by my father for emergencies rolled in my stocking, I tried to hide my elation from my parents.

Acknowledgments

Grateful acknowledgment is given to the authors and publishers listed below for brief passages excerpted from these longer works.

from *Woman in the Mists: The Story of Dian Fossey and the Mountain Gorillas of Africa* by Farley Mowat. Copyright © 1987 by Farley Mowat Limited. Warner Books.

from *Summer of My German Soldier* by Bette Greene. Copyright © 1973 by Bette Greene. Puffin Books.

from *Lift Every Voice* by Dorothy Sterling and Benjamin Quarles. Copyright © 1965 by Doubleday & Company. Zenith Books.

from *Trial by Ice* by K. M. Kostyal. Copyright © 1999 by the National Geographic Society.

from *Norby and the Oldest Dragon* by Janet and Isaac Asimov. Copyright © 1990 by Janet and Isaac Asimov. Ace Books.

from *The Great Interactive Dream Machine* by Richard Peck. Copyright © 1996 by Richard Peck. Dial Books for Young Readers.

from *An Ocean Apart, a World Away* by Lensey Namioka. Copyright © 2002 by Lensey Namioka. Delacorte Press.

from *The Buried City of Pompeii* by Shelley Tanaka. Copyright © 1997 by the Madison Press Limited. Madison Press Books.

from *Turn of the Century* by Nancy Smiler Levinson. Copyright © 1994 by Nancy Smiler Levinson. Lodestar Books, an affiliate of Dutton Children's Books.

from *Keepers and Creatures at the National Zoo* by Peggy Thomson. Copyright © 1988 by Peggy Thomson. Thomas Y. Crowell.

from *Mountain Light* by Laurence Yep. Copyright ©1985 by Laurence Yep. Harper & Row.

from *On the Bus with Joanna Cole: A Creative Autobiography* by Joanna Cole, with Wendy Saul. Copyright © 1996 by Joanna Cole. Heinemann.

from *Eleanor Roosevelt: A Life of Discovery* by Russell Freedman. Copyright © 1993 by Russell Freedman. Clarion Books, an imprint of Houghton Mifflin.

from *Behind Barbed Wire: The Imprisonment of Japanese Americans During World War II* by Daniel S. Davis. Copyright © 1982 by Daniel S. Davis. E. P. Dutton.

from *So Big* by Edna Ferber. Copyright © 1924 and renewed 1952 by Edna Ferber. University of Illinois Press.

from *A Long Hard Journey: The Story of the Pullman Porter* by Patricia and Frederick McKissack. Copyright © 1989 by Patricia and Frederick McKissack. Walker & Company.

from *Sally Ride: America's First Woman in Space* by Carolyn Blacknall. Copyright ©1984 by Carolyn Blacknall. Dillon Press.

from "Appetizer" from *Ghost Traps* by Robert H. Abel. Copyright © 1991 by Robert H. Abel. University of Georgia Press.

from "My Mother and Father" from *The Leaving and Other Stories* by Budge Wilson. Copyright © 1990 by Budge Wilson. Philomel Books.

from *Matilda* by Roald Dahl. Copyright © 1988 by Roald Dahl. Puffin Books.

from *Snake's Daughter* by Gail Hosking Gilberg. Copyright © 1997 by the University of Iowa Press.

from *Now Is Your Time!* by Walter Dean Myers. Copyright © 1991 by Walter Dean Myers. HarperCollins Publishers.

from *The Kidnapped Prince: The Life of Olaudah Equiano* by Olaudah Equiano, adapted by Ann Cameron. Copyright © 1995 by Ann Cameron. Alfred A. Knopf.

from "Prime Time" from *Colored People* by Henry Louis Gates Jr. Copyright © 1994 by Henry Louis Gates Jr. Alfred A. Knopf, a division of Random House.

from *Dolphin Man: Exploring the World of Dolphins* by Laurence Pringle. Copyright © 1995 by Laurence Pringle. Atheneum Books for Young Readers.

from *Marie Curie* by Angela Bull. Copyright © 1986 by Angela Bull. Hamish Hamilton.

from "An Occurrence at Owl Creek Bridge" by Ambrose Bierce from *The Twilight Zone Companion* by Marc Scott Zicree. Copyright © 1982 by Marc Scott Zicree.

from *Charlotte Brontë and Jane Eyre* by Stewart Ross. Copyright © 1997 by Stewart Ross. Viking.

from *Robots Rising* by Carol Sonenklar. Copyright © 1999 by Carol Sonenklar. Henry Holt and Company.